IDENTITY:
THE FOUNDATION
OF THE CITY

HENRI LEVAVASSEUR

IDENTITY

THE FOUNDATION OF THE CITY

RECONCILING ETHNOS AND POLIS

ARKTOS
LONDON 2025

ARKTOS

🌐 Arktos.com ❋ fb.com/Arktos ◐ ◎ arktosmedia ✉ arktosjournal

Copyright © 2025 by Arktos Media Ltd. and La Nouvelle Librairie.

All rights reserved. No part of this book may be reproduced or utilised in any form or by any means (whether electronic or mechanical), including photocopying, recording or by any information storage and retrieval system, without permission in writing from the publisher.

L'identité, socle de la cité: Réconcilier Ethnos et Polis, published as part of the *Collection Cartouches* by La Nouvelle Librairie éditions in 2021.

ISBN
978-1-917646-67-3 (Paperback)
978-1-917646-68-0 (Ebook)

Translation
Roger Adwan

Editing
Constantin von Hoffmeister

Layout and Cover
Tor Westman

CONTENTS

Foreword: Rather Big Father than Big Other vii

I. The Dawn of a Modern Nation 1

II. Liberal Aporia.. 15

III. Thinking in *Ethnos*-Based Terms......................... 29

Conclusion: Re-Becoming What We Are 43

❦

L'Institut Iliade for Long European Memory.................... 51

ξεῖνε, τὸ μέν σε πρῶτον ἐγὼν εἰρήσομαι αὐτή
τίς πόθεν εἰς ἀνδρῶν; πόθι τοι πόλις ἠδὲ τοκῆες;

'Stranger, this question will I myself ask thee first.
Who art thou among men, and from whence?
Where is thy city, and where thy parents?'

— HOMER, *Odyssey*, Book XIX

'Even the beauty of a race or family, its charm
and grace in all its demeanour, has to be worked for:
just like genius, it is the final result of the accumulated
work of generations.'

— FRIEDRICH NIETZSCHE, *Twilight of the Idols*

FOREWORD

RATHER BIG FATHER THAN BIG OTHER

Konk¹'s most famous cartoon is the one where two Martians—with their big ears and antennae—are talking. 'So, we're French too?' asks the first; to which the second replies, 'Well, of course we are, everyone is French!' Such is indeed the doctrine of a Europe without borders and a nationality code that gives pride of place to the right of soil and individual interests. This, however, is not Henri Levavasseur's opinion! In truth, those two nice Martians fail to fulfil several criteria of belonging: they are not, first of all, of terrestrial origin; nor do they participate in life on Earth. In short, they share neither our *ethnos* nor our *polis*.

And yet, the great civilisational upheaval imposed upon us upsets all balances: the European Union aims to define itself as being without geographical boundaries, without commercial limits, without human borders, and without any cultural definition; the Republic, which we no longer dare call French, aspires to impose a contractual and ideological conception of the homeland—a 'living together' that is, in fact, anything but that, in the absence of any *affectio societatis* between indifferent, if not hostile, communities. And it is Henri Levavasseur who sets the record straight and puts the church in the middle of the

---

1   Translator's note (TN): Konk is a famous French illustrator.

village: first, through a reasoned rereading of Renan's famous text entitled *What Is a Nation?* Contrary to contemporary exegesis, Renan never claimed that race, language, culture, history, religious affinities, material interests, and military necessities did not matter. Quite to the contrary, he devoted extensive discussion to these aspects so as to emphasise their importance, but simply considered these necessary conditions to be insufficient. Renan thus defined the nation as a spiritual principle, rooted in the heritage of a common history and the desire to build a common destiny. The will to live together is therefore an indispensable element of the existence of a civic nation, i.e. that of a *polis*. It is, however, identity that remains the very foundation of the city.

A shared future can only take shape when one draws on one's deep roots.

Nevertheless, and contrary to all common sense, the prophets and clergymen of 'republican values' strive to exclude from our national identity anything that sets the French apart from peoples who come from other civilisations. It is a death trap, for France cannot be reduced to two centuries of the Republic. France is a line of forty kings; one thousand years of history stretching back to the coronation of Hugh Capet;[2] fifteen centuries dating back to the baptism of Clovis,[3] which represents the founding act of the Frankish kingdom's resumption of its Roman heritage. And when one examines the monuments devoted to the heroes that fell during the two world wars, one does not encounter the words 'died for the Republic', but, instead, 'died for France'.

As for the European Union, it will only cease to be a bureaucratic burden (thus becoming a true *polis*) once it inscribes itself into a long-term vision. As Charles de Gaulle expressed it in his *Memoirs of Hope*:

---

2   TN: Hugh Capet was the King of the Franks from 987 to 996.
3   TN: Clovis was the first king to unite all of the Franks under one single ruler. He is thus considered to be the founder of the Merovingian dynasty.

With all [the nations of Europe] being part of the same white race, the same Christian origins and the same way of life, linked to one another since time immemorial by countless ties of thought, art, science, politics and trade, it is in accordance with their very nature that they should come together and form one whole that has its own character and organisation in relation to the rest of the world.[4]

Henri Levavasseur thus advocates a swing of the pendulum. Indeed, we must break out of the Enlightenment cycle and the illusions of a universal Republic and a globalist European Union. We must relearn to organise ourselves into organic, cohesive communities based on the *ethnos* of our origins and our way of being, on our civilisational *ethos*. We must remain faithful to the heritage of our ancestors, at the expense of our openness to others if necessary. In short, what we must do is prefer *Big Father* to *Big Other*.

JEAN-YVES LE GALLOU

---

4   Author's note (AN): Charles de Gaulle, *Memoirs of Hope*, Volume 1, Plon, Paris, 1970, pages 181–182.

CHAPTER I

THE DAWN OF A MODERN NATION

What Is a Nation? Rereading Renan

FOR THE proponents of 'republican' historiography, belonging to a nation is primarily reduced to a kind of contractual will expressed by individuals of different origins who share a strong desire to 'live together'. From this perspective, it is customary to refer to the famous lecture entitled 'What Is a Nation?', which Ernest Renan delivered at the Sorbonne on 11 March 1882. Most contemporary exegetes of this text readily contrast Renan's definition of the nation with a supposedly 'essentialist' vision of identity, one that is said to be more or less rooted in the tradition of Fichte's *Addresses to the German Nation*.[1] In the eyes of the acolytes of republican orthodoxy, the latter tradition is basically suspected of inevitably leading to racism, an intrinsically criminal or criminogenic ideology. One thus forgets a little too quickly that Fichte, the father of German idealism, who was both Kant's disciple and one of Schelling's inspirations, was—just as much as Renan—a 'child of the Enlightenment'. Above all, however, this constitutes a serious misuse of Renan's text, as one attributes to the author intentions he never had,

---

1   AN: Johann Gottlieb Fichte, *Addresses to the German Nation*. Translation by Léon Philippe, Delagrave, Paris, 1895.

as can readily be gathered from a careful reading of the 1882 conference. While Renan notes that the genesis of a nation is a complex and long-term phenomenon, one that results from a melting pot in which diverse components merge, he does not necessarily conclude that 'diversity' is, in all its forms and proportions, a quality in itself. In contrast with such simplistic and abusive interpretations, it is thus appropriate, despite Renan's polemical aims, which were connected with the 'spirit of the times', to do justice to the finesse and nuance that characterised Renan's thought.

To be properly analysed, the purpose of Renan's lecture must, of course, be re-placed in its original context, namely that of the 'revanchist' patriotism of the Third Republic. Having had a dewy-eyed fondness for Germanic thought since the beginning of the Romantic era, the French intelligentsia, now mortified by the humiliation suffered in 1871, rejected almost anything originating from across the Rhine, without, however, being able to rid itself of a certain fascination for German historical science and philological scholarship, both of which were forged in one of the most prestigious university systems in Europe. To the French republicans, who had barely averted the risk of monarchical restoration in 1873, it was all a matter of uniting the country around an ideal that could reconcile the memory of past French glories with democratic mystique, in a desire to counter the dynamism of the young Teutonic nation. Indeed, the latter had managed to achieve a fruitful synthesis between tradition and modernity, combining economic, industrial, and scientific growth with the preservation of aristocratic social structures, the maintenance of a monarchical political system, and the claim to an unbroken continuity with its old Germanic heritage. French Republicans also had to curb their ideological hostility towards religion in order to protect the opinion of the Catholic faithful that they were initially seeking to win over: the time had not yet come to openly attack the Church once again, as had been the case in the heyday of the Convention.[2] This manoeuvre was, incidentally, destined to be completely successful: in 1892, a hundred years after the September massacres in the prisons of Terror,[3] Catholics would succumb to the 'rallying' illusion desired by Pope Leo XIII, which did not in any way prevent the Republic from promulgating the law that would separate Church and State in 1905.

Renan's text bears the very mark of such ambiguities; what it reflects, above all, is a constant concern to refute a certain 'German' conception of the nation, one which is based on the notion of a very ancient community of blood and language that is destined to appropriate a geographical space commensurate with its own demographic expansion. Hence Renan's initial insistence on minimising the significance that one should grant ethnic data, even though he would then stress the latter's importance in the final part of his lecture; not to mention his emphasis on the diversity of the origins that characterise the peoples that make up modern nations—a diversity which was, however, quite relative, since in Renan's time, it remained limited to Celtic, Latin, and Germanic contributions.

Similarly, the author emphasises the little regard one should have for religion when defining national unity, although he does not fail to highlight the importance of Christianity in the genesis of the French nation. Last but not least, Renan champions a certain form of distrust of historical knowledge, one that could threaten the credibility of the 'national narrative' (an expression which he does not, however, use in this actual lecture): according to him, the coherence of this 'narrative' presupposes a generous dose of forgetfulness. In this regard, we are a

---

2   TN: The National Convention (*Convention nationale*) was the constituent assembly of the Kingdom of France for one day and that of the First French Republic for the first three years of the French Revolution.

3   TN: This is a reference to the Reign of Terror (*la Terreur*), a period of the French Revolution that followed the creation of the First Republic, when a series of massacres and numerous public executions took place in response to Federalist revolts, revolutionary fervour, anticlerical sentiment, and accusations of treason by the Committee of Public Safety.

million miles away from our contemporary culture of repentance, a repentance that makes it impossible for the nation to reconcile itself with its own history. One might, of course, object, stating that today's most virulent attacks against our 'national narrative' stem from genuine ideological manipulation rather than rigorous historical research; but could Renan have foreseen, back in his day, the devastation wrought in our time and age by a truly hysterical process of collective guilt founded on a relentlessly biased rewriting of the past?

In the first two parts of his lecture, Renan's argumentation is, in fact, entirely inspired by the desire to challenge the legitimacy of the annexation of Alsace and a part of Lorraine by imperial Germany. None of the following, according to Renan, could suffice to establish the rights of nations: not the argument of dynastic continuity (to which France could no longer lay claim), nor the reminder of the violence committed in the past ('unity is always achieved through brutal means,' he writes); not the argument of race (insofar as political boundaries do not necessarily correspond to ethnic boundaries), nor that of language (Renan mentions the example of Switzerland); not that of religion ('which has become an individual matter; [...] almost entirely removed from the reasons that delineate the boundaries of peoples'), nor that of common economic interest ('a *Zollverein*[4] is not a homeland') or that of natural geographical boundaries ('mountains cannot divide states').

Refusing to accept any 'fait accompli'[5] policy, Renan then proceeds to outline what, to him, constitutes the founding principle of national sovereignty:

> ...[I]t is not the land any more than the race that makes a nation. The land provides the substrate, the field of struggle and labour, and it is man that

---

4   TN: Customs Union.
5   TN: This French expression, used as is in the English language, means 'done deal' or something that cannot be changed.

provides the soul. Man is everything in the formation of this sacred thing we call a people.

To Renan, people and nation are therefore one and the same! The author knows that this has not always been the case: the ancient City and imperial Rome were not nations in the modern sense of the term. Strangely enough, the author here pays homage to the decisive historical role of the Germans in the founding of future modern states:

It was the Germanic invasion that introduced the world to the principle that would later serve as a basis for the existence of nationalities.

The adoption of Christianity by Germanic peoples then facilitated their merging with the indigenous populations among whom they had settled: '...over the centuries, the mould they imposed became the very mould of the nation.' And the Franks would ultimately give their name to the kingdom that had been born from their efforts.

The Modern Nation: An Obsolete Model?

If nations have not always existed, they are also not a reality that prevails everywhere: 'Why is Holland a nation, whereas Hanover and the Grand Duchy of Parma are not?' In the third part of his lecture, Renan provides the answer to this question by defining the nation as a 'spiritual principle' to which he attributes two sources, one located in the past, the other in the present: on the one hand, 'the shared possession of a rich legacy of memories,' and on the other, 'present consent, the desire to live together, and the will to continue to assert the heritage that one has received in undivided form.' The famous notion of an 'everyday plebiscite', on which Renan bases the existence of the nation, is therefore inconceivable without the legacy of a shared past and without a strong awareness of having common roots. Reading the rest of the text confirms this interpretation:

> Man [...] cannot be improvised. The nation, just like the individual, is the culmination of a long history of effort, sacrifice and devotion. Ancestor worship is more legitimate than anything else, for it was our ancestors that

made us the way we are. [...] Having common glories in the past, a common will in the present; having done great things together, and wanting to do more: these are the essential conditions for being a people. [...] We love the house we have built and passed on. The Spartan chant "We are what you were and shall be what you are" is, in its simplicity, the abbreviated anthem of every homeland.

It is obvious that the 'will to uphold the heritage', which constitutes the keystone of what Renan calls a 'nation', presupposes a heritage that can be passed on.

> Man is everything in the formation of this sacred thing we call a people. Nothing material could be sufficient. A nation is a spiritual principle, resulting from the profound complications of history, a spiritual family.

Renan would undoubtedly not have contradicted Jean Mabire,[6] for whom peoples 'have been shaped by thousands of years of prolonged patience'.[7]

We can thus clearly see that this is all a fragile sort of alchemy, and Renan is under no illusions about it when he writes:

> One could say that secession and, in the long run, the fragmentation of nations are the consequence of a system that places these old organisms at the mercy of often unenlightened wills. [...] Human wills change; but what doesn't down here? Nations are not eternal. They have a beginning, and so they shall have an end.

Renan even becomes a visionary when he attempts to discern the outlines of the order that shall, one day, replace the old nations: 'A European confederation will probably replace them.' Does this mean that Renan called for the establishment of a supranational entity based

---

6 TN: Having authored more than a hundred published works, Jean Mabire was a neo-pagan and nordicist who was also active as a journalist and essayist.

7 AN: Jean Mabire, *La Torche et le glaive — L'écrivain, la politique et l'espérance* [TN: The Torch and the Sword — The Writer, Politics and Hope], Dualpha, Paris 2018.

on a universalist project that would abolish particular identities? This is quite uncertain, since he immediately asserts that nations remain, for the time being, 'a guarantee of freedom, a freedom that would be lost if the world had only one law and one master'.

Renan's lucidity seems to foreshadow Paul Valéry's words in his work entitled *The Crisis of the Mind*, published in 1919: 'We civilisations now know that we are mortal.' And yet, the acuity with which Renan analyses the genesis and destiny of the modern model of the nation does sometimes give way to strange bouts of naiveté, inspired by a type of philosophical idealism of which he cannot free himself, particularly when writing:

> ... [M]an is a reasonable and moral being, even before being confined to a particular language; before being a member of a particular race and adhering to a particular culture. Indeed, before French, German or Italian culture, there is human culture.

However, nowhere does such a 'human culture' predate the emergence of specific cultures. This is the whole meaning behind Joseph de Maistre's famous statement:

> There is no such thing as man in this world. I have seen French people, Italians, and Russians; and thanks to Montesquieu, I even know that one can be Persian; but as for man, I declare never to have encountered him in my life; and if he does indeed exist, it is unbeknownst to me.[8]

Dominique Venner writes something similar:

> Men exist in their diversity only through what distinguishes them, namely clans, peoples, nations, cultures, and civilisations, and not through what they superficially have in common. Only their animalism is universal.[9]

---

8 AN: Joseph de Maistre, *Considérations sur la France* [TN: Thoughts on France], London, 1797, page 102.

9 AN: Dominique Venner, *Un samouraï d'Occident. Le bréviaire des insoumis* [TN: A Samurai of the West — A Breviary of the Unsubjugated], Pierre-Guillaume de Roux, Paris, 2013, p. 292.

Just as a tree cannot do without its roots, the universal exists only as a polyphonic extension of specific identities. Having passed away in 1892, Renan could not have foreseen the upheavals of the 'century of 1914' (to borrow the title of a work by Dominique Venner[10]). He could not have imagined what would come next: the suicide of European nations in the hell of the two world wars; the crumbling of their supremacy over other continents; the spiritual distress of these nations in the grip of doubt and the questioning of their traditional value system; the triumph of a liberal sort of model, which would lead to the atomisation of national communities into an aggregate of individuals endowed with 'universal' rights; the neglecting of the 'long memory' of peoples and its replacement by a selective memory, one that is geared towards what denies them and destroys their very souls; the arrival of waves of populations and other civilisations from other continents, all in the space of a few decades, followed by the brutal intrusion of Islam into societies that had long been Christian... No historian has better assessed the far-reaching consequences of this generalised disaster than Jean de Viguerie, in a remarkable work entitled *Les Deux Patries*[11]:

Echoing Nietzsche's declaration that 'God is dead', Viguerie issues a dire warning: it is our old fatherland that is dead — killed by the revolutionary homeland. Indeed, the author establishes a radical distinction between the ancestral fatherland, the 'land of the fathers', and the more recent homeland, stemming from revolutionary ideology: 'The latter is not France, yet France is its support and its instrument.' This philosophical homeland, heir to liberalism and certain cosmopolitan currents of the Enlightenment, aspires to replace the old physical fatherlands with its purely ideological vision of the nation: to

---

10 AN: Dominique Venner, *Le Siècle de 1914. Utopies, guerres et révolutions en Europe au xxe siècle* [TN: The Century of 1914 — Utopias, Wars and Revolutions in 20th-Century Europe], Pygmalion, Paris, 2006.

11 AN: Jean de Viguerie, *Les Deux Patries. Essai historique sur l'idée de France et de Patrie* [TN: The Two Fatherlands — A Historical Essay on the Notion of France and the Fatherland], 2nd edition, Dominique Martin Morin, Bouère, 2003.

the 'citizens of the world', 'the homeland is wherever one feels good', and France's vocation is to be at the forefront of this emancipation movement; the new type of man, embodied by the republican citizen, must help humanity move 'from shadow to light'.

Viguerie's analysis goes far beyond the Maurrasian opposition between one's 'real country' and the 'legal country'. Not only does he criticise Maurras's integral nationalism ('France alone') for sinking into an anti-Germanism whose excesses are ultimately reminiscent of revolutionary Manichaeism (Germany, Maurras declares, 'has broken with the tradition of the human race'), but, above all, draws a terrifying conclusion that highlights the fundamental incompatibility between the revolutionary homeland and the land of the fathers, with the calls for a 'sacred union' issued during World War I doomed to remain futureless, and thus as illusory as the exhortations to 'unity' uttered by contemporary leaders, all of whom are powerless to protect their people against terrorist acts perpetrated by individuals who have entered the national territory in blatant defiance of the law. Viguerie no longer believed in the possibility of the national revival that Maurras had so fervently hoped for; to him, we are now faced with chaos:

> ...the now vanished fatherland, our inconsistent nation, and a State that exhausts our last remaining strength. How could France still endure, when we are watching it die before our eyes? We can but declare it deceased.

In this regard, Viguerie denies being pessimistic, insofar as lucidity is essential as a prerequisite for any potential renewal:

> As long as we obscure reality, ambiguity will persist. [...] There is, in fact, no France anymore, and it is those in power who have killed it. [...] It is, after all, high time we all knew who we are dealing with here: formidable enemies, who already have the destruction of the fatherland under their belts. [...] We cannot save a France that no longer exists. We might, however, be able to prevent or delay further destruction [...] while anticipating the formation of a new political association worthy of such a name."

---

12   AN: Ibid, p. 283.

Is France Dead?

The 'France that is no more', as referred to by Viguerie, should not be confused with the state that bears the same name today: there is indeed a political entity called France, which retains most of the attributes of sovereign power within the territory corresponding to that of the former French fatherland, possesses nuclear weapons, and holds a permanent seat on the United Nations Security Council. Many French people still living on its soil continue to consider it their duty, and perhaps rightly so, to defend this political entity and help preserve what remains of its power, believing that it is particularly important not to leave this power in hostile and foreign hands. From the ancient French fatherland, this state has also inherited its language, its landscapes, and some rather prestigious relics bequeathed by our previous generations—what is now commonly referred to as our 'heritage'. All of this is not to be disregarded. However, this political entity appears quite distinct from the old, physical fatherland: its population is now divided into adverse parts, simply because it no longer constitutes a people, but rather a group of citizens who have little common history. It is certainly no longer the France of the *Ancien Régime*,[13] but also no longer Renan's France, nor even that of the early years of the Fifth Republic. In the space of barely two generations, the face of France has profoundly and radically changed—a finding agreed on by those who deplore this situation and those who welcome it alike. In both its magnitude and its suddenness, such an upheaval, corresponding to an equally profound change in the composition of our population, is unprecedented in the history of our country.

However, the old France may not have given up the ghost yet, despite the terrible observation made by Jean de Viguerie. The existence of the traditional fatherland is undoubtedly no longer evident to a large number of the inhabitants of our 'Hexagon'. And it is certainly

---

13 TN: Meaning the political and social system in France before the Revolution of 1789.

no longer visible to everyone, but has it not simply found refuge in the secrecy of our hearts, in the recesses of our memories and the depths of our ancient lands? In the beautiful words of Maurice Barrès,[14] the earth and the dead have become its kingdom, which is no longer entirely of this world. Although this France, one that is almost secret today, has entered a long winter of slumber, all those who have not forgotten it still feel the warmth of its breath. They feel her tutelary presence and sometimes recognise her face in the features of a certain uncle from Picardy, a certain cousin from Anjou, or a certain friend from Provence. Was she not, in her days of splendour, already heir to all the 'nursing mothers' who faithfully watched over our woods and fields before her time, in the days of our German, Latin, and Celtic ancestors, and of all those who preceded them since the dawn of time?

In truth, two worlds co-exist within our borders, but is it not the same case elsewhere in Europe? One need only travel from a Cotswold hamlet to the streets of London, from the Lüneburg Heath to certain cities in the Ruhr region, or from a village in Abruzzo to the suburbs of a major Italian city to understand that this retreat from our physical homelands is evident everywhere. So much so that we may be witnessing a phenomenon of much greater magnitude than that described by Jean de Viguerie with regard to France alone: perhaps it all represents the completion of a long historical cycle, of which the existence of modern nations is but the ultimate stage, one that precedes a new and decisive period in the destiny of our civilisation.

To grasp the full scope of the great civilisational upheaval that the peoples of Europe are currently facing, it is worth reflecting on the expression of two concepts forged more than 2,500 years ago, in the brilliance of the dawn of Greek thought: *polis* (πόλις) and *ethnos* (ἔθνος). While the former term is an essentially geographical concept, designating a given space organised by its inhabitants (cf. the Indo-European root *tpelH-, 'fortification') and meaning 'city' (and by

---

14 TN: Auguste-Maurice Barrès was a French novelist, journalist, philosopher, and deputy of the French National Assembly.

extension, a 'gathering of citizens', a 'state'), the latter word applies to a human community defined not by a territory, but by its origins and the traditions that distinguish it: *ethnos* is etymologically related to the noun *ethos* (ἔθος, and its extended variant ἦθος), meaning 'custom', 'convention', or, in terms of verbs, *ethó* (ἔθω), i.e. 'to be accustomed to', derived from the Indo-European *swe-d^{h}h1-, 'to make one's own' (cf. the Sanskrit term *svádhā*, 'custom', 'habit', and the Latin word *sodalis*, meaning 'companion' or 'friend').

In the Greek world, the *polis* was not at odds with the *ethnos*: it certainly represented a particular form of organisation and was confined to a limited space, but it did not arise from an abstract construction created *ex nihilo*, beyond any connection to a given *ethnos*. On a completely different scale, this is also the case with the modern nation model described by Renan at the end of the 19th century: while its genesis is based on a very long history that brought together elements of much more diverse origins than the population of ancient cities, which had been founded by a limited number of families or clans, the nation mentioned by Renan did nonetheless emerge from a fusion of almost exclusively European contributions, of people who often shared comparable customs, retaining through and through the mark of a Christian civilisation erected upon an ancient, immemorial pagan foundation. Although certainly never unchanging but rather subject to constant evolution, this age-old balance does rest upon fundamental anthropological structures that have never been irremediably altered, until an attempt to radically subvert the entire system of traditional values, in combination with a mass arrival of non-European populations, triggered a twofold trauma during the last decades of the 20th century, the consequences of which have not yet been fully apprehended by most of our contemporaries.

The disunion between *ethnos* and *polis* seems well and truly complete today, so much so that, in large portions of its territory, the nation (a word derived from the Latin *natio*, i.e. 'offspring', 'spawn', 'people', just as the term *patria* refers to the land of the forefathers) only brings together an aggregation of 'citizens', some of whom—most often people of native origin—are deprived of any memory of identity, while others gather into communities knit around a more and more clearly asserted ethno-cultural identity, an identity that is, however, very different to the one that the host country possessed a few decades earlier. All these individuals, citizens of a now fractured nation, are less driven by the desire to 'live together' than by the necessity to 'live side by side'. By virtue of the principle of heterotelia[15] and through the stubborn denial of the identity of the physical homeland, the republican discourse on the unity of the nation has, in a matter of a few years, resulted instead in the erosion of 'republican' cohesion and the resurgence of ethnicity-based 'community' sentiments: the significance of the *ethnos*, the reality of which some have strived to deny in favour of a revolutionary conception of the *polis* now stripped of any and all identity, is now evident to everyone, especially to short-term French citizens, who are all determined not to renounce their extra-European cultural roots.

---

15 TN: Heterotelia refers to the fact of having the purpose of one's existence or occurrence outside of, or apart from, oneself.

CHAPTER II

LIBERAL APORIA

'Hexagonalism' — The Terminal Stage of the Republic

PARALYSED BY the realisation of their own powerlessness in the face of the gigantic size of the wave gradually taking shape before their eyes, the political leaders, economic elites and high clergy of our fashionable intellectuals have no other choice but to surrender to a headlong rush into a genuine denial of reality. This little world thus continues to reduce national cohesion to mere 'hexagonalism', wherein the ritual invocation of the 'values of the Republic' is expected to constitute the ultimate guarantor of our unity. Having become universal, however, these very values cannot be considered specifically French, unless it is because of our compatriots' claim to have been their originators. The appeals made by the authorities to 'reject the secession' of a certain part of the 'Republic's territories' come across as very strange indeed, when one considers the fact that the Republic was forged specifically through the manifestation of a desire for brutal secession from the old France, as evidenced by the 'extermination law' passed by the Convention on 1 October 1793, by the explicit orders given at the time by the Committee of Public Safety, as well as by the letters of various generals and representatives of the Convention detailing the zealous fulfilment of their mission in Vendée, Nantes and Lyon.

Similarly, when today's fanatics resort to knives to practice beheadings in our streets, how can we not shudder with horror as we recall the serial throat-slitting carried out in Parisian prisons during the massacres of September 1792? How can we forget the death of the Princess of Lamballe, who was slaughtered by these same 'Septembriseurs'[1] and her body dragged by the crowd towards a boundary marker, on which her head was placed. A man called Grison then sawed it off with his knife and placed it on the end of a pike, while the wigmaker Charlat cut open the corpse's chest to tear out the heart and place it on the tip of his sabre. It is worth remembering that these abominations were not committed by the criminal dregs of the population, but most often by honest Parisian petty bourgeois, whose crimes were justified after the fact by the authorities of the time, all in the name of the salvation of the Republic!

It could indeed be the case that the very model of the modern nation, which, in the aftermath of the bloody cataclysm of the French Revolution, has gradually been spreading across Europe over the past two centuries, is actually already doomed, even if today's nations continue to exist in the eyes of international law. Based on an abstract conception of citizenship consistent with the liberal ideas of the Enlightenment, this political model only succeeded in taking real historical shape by grafting itself onto specific and pre-existing political entities tied to an ethno-cultural substratum that had slowly taken form over the centuries. And it is this substratum that the modern nation has gradually drained of its substance by imposing a new ideological framework, one which wreaks destruction upon all historical continuity and ultimately leaves peoples unable to prevent their own disappearance. In the more or less long term, this phenomenon will, in turn, lead the nation towards an inevitable downfall.

Mutatis mutandis, this situation is reminiscent of the end of the Soviet world, whose Marxist ideology seemed to impose itself upon

---

1   TN: A French term which refers to anyone that participated in, or supported, the September massacres.

all the peoples it controlled: for citizens living east of the Iron Curtain, there seemed to be no other possibility but collectivism, until the day when the regime collapsed like a house of cards, simply because its ideology was based on words and concepts that no longer had anything to do with reality: overnight, what had seemed self-evident and untouchable became an object of ridicule and utter rejection. Liberal democracy could one day suffer the very same fate, with the fundamental difference that its disappearance will lead to much greater chaos than that of the end of the *Ordo Sovieticus*, which, incidentally, has made way for the reawakening of old interethnic conflicts whose undercurrents had persisted in Eastern Europe. What will happen tomorrow in a Western Europe subject to inner division as a result of the presence of communities that are radically alien to its history and customs, while indigenous populations are deprived of the very awareness of their own identity? The headlong rush of republican ideology is strikingly similar to that of the communist world: if Marxist society functions poorly, it is because it is not yet Marxist enough, proclaimed the leaders east of the Iron Curtain; if multicultural society does not function, it is because we do not yet sufficiently adhere to the principles of our tolerant republic, which should be even more open to the world, proclaim the followers of the fashionable creed of the 'free world'.

Whatever the outcome of the coming crises, they will lead the peoples of Europe to resort to other resources than referring to outdated values and political systems that are unsuited to current challenges. What forms of political, economic, and social organisation will prevail then is anyone's guess. We can only be certain of one thing: nothing will ever be 'the same again'. If our old nations do end up surviving, however, it will be because they have been able to renounce in time the illusions of the 'republican pact' and have rediscovered an articulation of the *ethnos* and the *polis* that is more favourable to the expression of their own genius. If this is not the case, our peoples will have to adopt new means of political organisation capable of ensuring their longevity—for although the State *can* sometimes succeed in forging a people from diverse elements, peoples can also, for a time, manage very well without a State. Whatever the case, the future will necessarily have to be built on different principles than those that have brought us to the very brink of the abyss. Great upheavals can sometimes bring about salutary awakenings, as evidenced by this poet's words: 'Wherever danger lies, however, salvation also grows.'[2] The threat of future migration waves may well trigger the required earthquake for the dormant peoples of Europe to come to their senses. What seems out of reach today may thus well become possible. The acceleration of history and the convergence of catastrophes will, in any case, lead to unforeseen developments.

In the foreword to the second edition of *Deux Patries*, Jean de Viguerie delivers a vibrant appeal for us never to give up:

> I do not see why the death of France should condemn us to inaction. What I see in it instead are pressing reasons for *action*. We must preserve our heritage and make it flourish. We must perpetuate the French language, transmit the customs of our social conventions, and keep the flame of our civilisation alive. Is this worth nothing? If France is now dying or dead, must we therefore cease to found families and raise children? Is that worth nothing? The city has disappeared, but living people subsist. [...] One must therefore live, and live all the more intensely, as the "culture of death" [...] is omnipresent.

Viguerie's words are therefore neither hopeless nor despairing. He does, however, encounter his limits in the form of a deliberate departure from any 'political' horizon, insofar as his vision of the communities that are called to 'preserve the heritage' seems exclusively based on the practice of Christian virtues:

> ...what does it mean to live? It is to conduct ourselves as human beings endowed with reason and created in the image of God; it is for us to pray,

---

2   AN: Cf. Friedrich Hölderlin, Patmos, st. 1, v. 3–4: *'Wo aber Gefahr ist, wächst das Rettende auch.'* Cf. Gustave Roud's translation in *Hölderlin, Oeuvres* [TN: Hölderlin — Works] Gallimard, Paris, 1967, p. 867.

study, serve our loved ones, help the unfortunate, cultivate friendship, celebrate joyous events, and banish sadness and despair.

Although this advice is undoubtedly very sound, it can be applied at all times and in all places: being as universal as the Catholic faith and the mission of the Church, these principles tell us nothing about how to act to reconcile *ethnos* and *polis* so as to rebuild the City on lasting foundations. If the challenge is to preserve the existential conditions of our own ethno-cultural identity, it is important to define the latter in accordance with a fundamental anthropological reflection on the essence of human nature, for it constitutes the foundation on which we can develop an ethic or, in other words, a specific way of relating to the world, in harmony with the *mos majorum*, i.e. the customs established by our ancestors. It is this *ethos* that constitutes one of the foundations of our *ethnos*, based on which we will be able to reorganise the space of the *polis*: for although a people can certainly do without a state for a given amount of time, it cannot survive for long without taking on a 'political' form, without once again being in resonance with history. This is not about resorting to any kind of 'essentialism', in the sense of keeping our identity forever frozen in a more or less idealised representation of a certain bygone age, but rather about rediscovering the very momentum and tension that allowed our destiny as a people to blossom.

The City's Post-Modern Destruction

Meanwhile, the supporters of republican orthodoxy have divided the nation against itself by allowing millions of individuals of non-European origin to settle on its soil over the past half-century. Rather than acknowledge the dire consequences of their blindness, they actually have the audacity to call for 'unity' after each and every terrorist attack against our fellow citizens, as if it were somehow appropriate to ignore the perception of the social, ethnic, and cultural divides caused by decades of incompetence. While French people are, on a daily basis, urged to no longer advocate their belonging to the same historical community, a kind of 'communitarianism' inspired by cultures that are foreign to our traditions flourishes across entire swathes of the country. This phenomenon of 'communitarianism' has recently even been exploited by certain activists who do not shy away from using an oxymoron by defining themselves as 'natives of the Republic'. However, this 'indigenism' (by antiphrasis) cannot logically claim to have any republican character, since the Republic, in fact, only recognizes 'citizens', regardless of their origin and religious or ethnic affiliation. Moreover, the Republican authorities have not hesitated to convey that they disapprove of such discourse, which is likely to exacerbate tensions and, above all, to once again legitimise the use of the concept of 'race', which has become taboo—even if some 'indigenists' attempt to cloud the issue by asserting that this word does not refer to a biological reality, but rather to a 'social construct'. The authorities' discomfort is nonetheless palpable when feeling compelled to reprimand certain representatives of 'visible minorities': the latter are, of course, necessarily on the side of Good, to the extent that they enjoy a legitimacy inherent in having been victims of colonisation, a historical phenomenon recently described as a 'crime against humanity' by a 2017 presidential candidate visiting Algeria. During the same election campaign, this candidate also took pleasure in asserting that there was no such thing as 'French culture', but only a 'culture in France', one that is necessarily 'diverse' (sic). These words do not merely reflect the vision of a single man, who has since become head of state,[3] for they undoubtedly express an *opinio communis*, which is now shared by many contemporary politicians, senior officials, journalists, and intellectuals.

Moreover, in no way does the hostility to 'communitarianism' prevent the Republic from recognising the existence of another type of community, a community rooted not in one's adherence to a

---

3   TN: The man in question is none other than Macron.

given ethno-cultural identity, but in a display of certain behavioural preferences that are purely a matter of individual choice. These new communities proclaim themselves to be the holders of certain 'rights' and assert their presence in the public sphere, sometimes violently or provocatively, under the banner of radical feminism, homosexuality, trans-sexuality, and other forms of particularism—with the contents of this list not intended to be exhaustive in any way, of course. It should be noted that the purpose here is not for us to pass judgement on individual behaviour within the private sphere, but to highlight the ideological and eminently political nature of the struggle waged by groups claiming to speak in the name of a community of individuals characterised by their sexual orientation and practices—which is the only form of 'identity'-related belonging currently tolerated by the Republic. In passing, one should also bear in mind that this is a rather virulent form of essentialism, even though the proponents of this activism claim to fight against all forms of 'discrimination' and even strive to achieve the 'emancipation' of each and every person. However, it is likely that many homosexuals do not, in fact, identify with 'homosexualist' discourse, just as many women do not necessarily adhere to the feminist one.

In the name of the struggle against all forms of discrimination, 'clean slate' proponents undertake to 'deconstruct' the categories of classical anthropology, drawing, of course, on the 'postmodern' corpus of the leading thinkers of *French Theory*. First through media and social pressure, then by means of legal and statal coercion, they intend to impose, once and for all, the model of a 'fluid' identity, which is meant to replace 'natural' families and peoples, i.e. entities that are deemed oppressive or outdated.

The establishment of a 'marital institution for everyone' in various European countries constitutes an important step in this process of deconstruction, one whose aim is not so much to guarantee access to certain rights for everyone to enjoy as to modify the very nature of the institution of marriage from a deliberately subversive perspective:

ultimately, it is a matter of attacking the family model as a social unit based on hereditary transmission—with adoption having, up until now, only embodied a complementary mode of transmission, the existence of which did not call into question the 'natural' anthropological foundations on which the notion of filiation has always rested. By acknowledging the idea that marriage no longer serves to guarantee the continued existence of a family across generations, but only allows two people to unite and benefit from certain rights (including the right to have children or not, considered in this regard as an exclusively individual sort of aspiration, and not as the purpose of marriage as a 'political' institution, linked to the existence of the City), the concept of a 'marital institution for everyone' is part of a clearly liberal perspective. For the ideal of every liberal society is indeed that of an association of individuals who have the ability to freely choose their own identity, ridding themselves, where necessary, of hereditary and cultural determinisms. Such a society has, in fact, no need of a past and no need of a heritage (apart from the one that its fleeting whim incites it to embrace). It no longer needs to project itself into the future, either: all that matters is the necessity to guarantee, here and now, unfettered indulgence in one's enjoyment of 'natural' and universal rights. While this model has, up until now, distinguished itself from the communist totalitarianisms of the 20th century in terms of the means of persuasion used to force people to accept the questioning of their own historical existence, it nonetheless represents a considerable type of danger, since it leads, even more surely than communism itself, to genuine civilisational collapse: indeed, the atomisation of the social body, thus reduced to a mere mass of interchangeable consumers, results in the disappearance of all forms of authentic culture and consequently in a profound denaturing of human existence.

The Disunion of *Polis* and *Ethnos*

From a 'post-modern' liberal perspective, sovereign individuals must be able to construct themselves in complete autonomy. Social order thus no longer serves any other purpose but to guarantee the exercise of such free will. This *doxa* applies to the domain of sexual identity, where it becomes possible to postulate the existence of 'gender' categories completely independent of any biological realities. It also extends to the domain of the very identity of peoples and nations, both of which are thus reduced to an arbitrary construct whose nature is purely contractual, one in which the feeling of belonging to a single ethno-cultural community no longer has any place. This ideology represents the ultimate stage of the individualistic and contractual conception of society developed by certain Enlightenment thinkers. Such an evolution could undoubtedly not have been imagined in the 18th century by the 'founding fathers' of philosophical liberalism, convinced as they were of allowing themselves to be wisely guided by Reason alone. The fact remains, however, that the fracture caused by their 'rationalist' system of thought enabled the subsequent emergence of political and social upheavals whose scope and violence have been considerable. Indeed, even in its early days, liberal thought, which now asserts itself as intrinsically 'moderate' in contrast with all kinds of 'extremism', all of which it rejects with equal good conscience, embodied a profound break with earlier conceptions of human nature—although Chesterton[4] did define these new ideas as 'Christian virtues gone mad', and certain concepts of modern state theory do transpose secularised theological concepts into the non-religious sphere, as clearly demonstrated by Carl Schmitt.[5]

---

4   TN: In addition to being a journalist, magazine editor, and literary and art critic, Gilbert Keith Chesterton was an English author, philosopher, and Christian apologist.

5   AN: Carl Schmitt, *Political Theology*, translated by Jean-Louis Schlegel, Gallimard, Paris, 1988.

According to the liberal way of thinking, which Alain de Benoist flawlessly analysed in one of his recent works,[6] man is not defined primarily as a member of a community anchored in a specific historical reality (family, 'order', fatherland), but mainly as an abstract, autonomous individual detached from the contingent identity inherited from his predecessors, and as someone who enters into a contract with society with the intention of guaranteeing the exercise of his own 'natural' rights. In the 8th chapter of his *Second Treatise of Government*, published in 1690, John Locke states that a child 'is not born a subject of any government or country'. The ideological construct on which the idea of a social contract is based takes of course little account of the historical existence of organic communities. Here, one encounters the old contrast between the notions of community (*Gemeinschaft*) and society (*Gesellschaft*), a contrast well highlighted by the German sociologist Ferdinand Tönnies in a famous work published in 1887.[7]

Having reached the 'post-modern' stage of its evolution, the extension of the liberal model sanctifies the disunion between *polis* and *ethnos*, that is, between sovereignty and identity. This model represents the culmination of the system of the 'republican homeland', one that is based on a purely contractual and ideological conception of the fatherland: it thus constitutes both its apogee and its final phase. Although the republican homeland has never completely merged with the actual and physical fatherland, content instead with using the latter as 'its support and instrument' over a period of two centuries, as stated by Jean de Viguerie (see above, Chapter I), the republic is now in grave danger of collapsing upon the ruins of France, akin to a parasite that would not long survive the organism whose substance it has drained.

---

6   AN: Alain de Benoist, *Contre le libéralisme. La société n'est pas un marché* [TN: Against Liberalism — Society Is Not a Market], Éditions du Rocher, Monaco, 2019.

7   AN: Ferdinand Tönnies, *Gemeinschaft and Gesellschaft*, translated by Niall Bond and Sylvie Mesure, Presses universitaires de France, Paris, 2015.

Once all ties between sovereignty and identity have been severed, sovereignty inevitably escapes the body of the nation and ends up becoming the expression of a mosaic of individual demands. At the same time, since nature abhors a vacuum, the weakening of the nation logically ends up paving the way for the emergence of various forms of supra-national sovereignty, forms which, as predicted by Ernest Renan, would not necessarily be inclined to respect our genuine freedoms, which had hitherto been guaranteed through the exercise of national sovereignty (see above, Chapter I). In this domain, a systematic recourse to the universal morality of 'human rights' ultimately serves to undermine the very foundations of traditional political order, with the latter linked to the sovereignty of a people over its own territory.

This critical situation is obviously complicated by the massive presence of populations of non-European origin: by gradually imposing their customs, traditions and unique identity, these people are logically occupying the civilisational space left vacant by Europeans. And who could blame them? It is hardly possible, in fact, to identify, whether individually or collectively, with a homeland whose identity is reduced to abstract and universal principles. Brandishing 'values' whose expression appears increasingly outdated and using them as the sole instrument of their convictions, the republican authorities have nothing solid in the face of those who reject their model, nor anything to offer, especially to those who would like to assimilate into what remains of the French nation. Through long-term and sometimes painful efforts, it is undoubtedly possible, over the generations, for an expatriate community to blend into the melting pot of the host nation, provided that this community does not constitute a mass large enough to suddenly upset the demographic balance of the host country and that the cultures of the two populations in question share certain affinities from the very outset. History provides us with numerous examples of successful assimilation processes, most often involving human groups and peoples from the same civilisational space, as was the case during the settlement of French Huguenots in Prussia after the Revocation of the Edict of Nantes. Economic considerations also play a role in the process of assimilation of a foreign population. The Huguenots were an industrious and learned elite group, whose arrival contributed to strengthening the dynamism of the Prussian society into which they integrated; a situation that is, of course, different from that of most contemporary waves of migration.

Is collapse therefore inevitable? Well, it is likely that we have now entered a 'long civilisational winter', a process that will display all the aspects of gradual and slow death throes, as our country is shaken by some rather violent convulsive spasms. It is not impossible that the political entity called the 'French Republic' will continue to exist throughout this time, and that it will still be worth devoting some energy to in order to keep it as functional as possible, while ensuring above all else that we avoid relinquishing control to elements that are completely foreign to our desire to guarantee the sustainability of our ethno-cultural identity. However, it would be futile to continue placing our hopes in the ability of this entity to embody 'what we are'. Our duty dictates that we do not give in to such blameworthy blindness through intellectual laziness, conformism or cowardice. Our generation must now accept a decisive historical responsibility, without losing sight of the fact that it is faced with the necessity to defend, one inch at a time, the ramparts of an already occupied citadel whose command no longer belongs to us, while simultaneously preparing other positions from which future generations can reclaim our civilisational space and grant it a new form once *kairos* (or the 'right moment') arrives; a moment that none of us can predict or situate. In the meantime, we must form a vanguard, without ceasing to wage a rearguard battle. The same requirement is already imposed on the youth of other European nations, with whom unprecedented solidarity must be forged, thus allowing us all to preserve the identities of our peoples in full awareness of what unites us through each of them.

It is impossible to engage in such a struggle without first reverting to a clear vision of the world, which, along with courage, constitutes the primary condition for our freedom of action. This approach is necessarily based on a mental return to one's perennial sources, in harmony with a realistic anthropology that is free of all biases imposed upon us by two centuries of liberal 'humanism'.

It is also particularly crucial to break with the kind of idealism which stems from a twofold mistake that consists, on the one hand, in ignoring the fundamentally political dimension of human nature and, on the other, in only granting ethno-cultural heritage a limited role in the dynamic process of constructing individual and collective identities.

CHAPTER III

THINKING IN *ETHNOS*-BASED TERMS

The Anthropological Foundations of Identity[1]

IN CONTRAST to liberal ideology, we should base our conception of the collective identity of the City on realistic anthropology. The latter must particularly rest upon specific ethological lessons. The science of species-related behaviour teaches us that humans are not 'specialised beings': unlike animals, they do not innately possess the qualities that would allow them to spontaneously adapt to a given environment. Humans are born without claws or fur, and their instincts are poorly developed. In return, their horizons are less limited than those of animals, which remain closely tied to their biotope. As remarked by biologist Konrad Lorenz,[2] man is a 'specialist in non-specialisation', who possesses, however, a clear 'aptitude for youthfulness': what nature did not endow him with at birth, man acquires through learning

---

1 AN: The following pages reproduce, in revised form, the contents of a contribution published in *Pour un réveil européen. Nature, Excellence, Beauté* (TN: For a European Awakening : Nature, Excellence, Beauty [Arktos, 2023]), edited by Olivier Eichenlaub, Éditions de la Nouvelle Librairie, Paris, 2020.

2 AN: See Konrad Lorenz's *Studies in Animal and Human Behavior: Lessons from the Evolution of Behavioral Theory*, translated by Catherine and Pierre Fredet, Seuil, Paris, 1990.

and the work of his own hands, that is through what the Greeks called *techné*, i.e. 'technique'. The myth of Epimetheus, recounted by Plato in his *Protagoras* dialogue, perfectly illustrates this particularity, which represents both a shortcoming and a strength. Tasked by Zeus with distributing qualities and attributes among living beings, the Titan Epimetheus performs this task for animals, leaving nothing useful to humans, who remain vulnerable until Prometheus steals the divine fire for them. The sociologist and anthropologist Arnold Gehlen[3] expands on this ancient concept when he defines man as an 'incomplete being' that is unfinished at birth, which makes him 'open to the world': however ignorant in its cradle, a child gradually learns to dominate its environment and communicate with its peers thanks to the teachings provided by its own kind. Man is therefore a 'naturally cultural being' and consequently a social one.

The development of our intelligence is closely linked to the learning of a language, a language that acts as both heir and bearer of a culture that underpins our vision of the world and structures our very thinking. There is therefore no natural state whose existence precedes that of society, as believed by Hobbes (*Leviathan*, Chapter XIII, published in 1651), much less some abstract individuals with pre-existing universal rights that predate the 'social contract', as claimed by some thinkers of the Enlightenment.

The emergence of a culture is always intimately linked to a territory, which implies a notion of borders and boundaries: for every culture is the product of the history of a specific people, of a particular human group within a delimited geographical space. Borders and boundaries should, however, not be perceived as shackles that restrain us, but as conditions for the existence of human cultures in all their diversity. During his beautiful reflection on the high relief of the Acropolis representing the goddess Athena leaning over a border stone, Heidegger emphasised that a boundary is certainly 'not only outline and frame,

---

3   AN: Arnold Gehlen, *Man, His Nature and Place in the World*, as translated by Christian Sommer, Gallimard, Paris, 2021.

[...] the place where something stops. Boundary means that through which something is gathered into its ownmost aspect, in order to appear thereby in all its fullness'.[4]

No culture can evolve in the absence of social order and institutions. What follows from this is that, as stated by Aristotle,[5] 'the city exists by nature', and 'man is by nature a political animal'. A stateless person, adds Aristotle, incurs the reproaches expressed by Homer and targeting every 'tribeless, homeless, lawless' man. For man does not exist separately from others, in the manner of a Cartesian subject, before establishing a connection with the world: open to the world from the very outset, he is shaped by his inheritance of a specific culture, which, in turn, renders him capable of founding his own inner world.

This realistic conception of human nature, based on the teachings of an ancient wisdom supported by the discoveries of modern European science, is nowadays violently contested by the proponents of a new vision of man and society that is profoundly subversive and totalitarian. This death-dealing ideology, however, comes up against the walls of reality, both on the level of individuals and that of peoples: the progress made over the past few decades in terms of genetic research now makes it possible for us to identify the distant origins of a population using DNA extracted from human remains that, at times, are very old indeed. The results of these analyses indicate that most peoples stem from the interbreeding of different human groups, all, however, in accordance with methods and ratios that bestow upon each one of them a specific identity, making it impossible to reduce their history to a mere phenomenon of incessant interbreeding.

With regard to Europe, paleogeneticists have highlighted the presence of three ancestral populations: the oldest is that of indigenous

---

4   AN: Translation by Henri Levavasseur. For a complete French version of the text, see Martin Heidegger's *The Origin of Art and the Destination of Thinking*, translated by Jean-Louis Chrétien and Michèle Reifenrath, *L'Herne* number 45, 1983, p. 86.

5   AN: Aristotle, *Politics I*, 2.

hunter-gatherers (the bearers of a partially Neanderthal heredity that distinguishes them, in particular, from the populations of Africa), who, from the seventh millennium BC onwards, first mingled with farmers of Anatolian origin, and then, beginning in the fourth millennium, with several waves of conquerors arriving from the southern steppes of present-day Russia.[6] And it was probably the latter who imposed, wherever they settled, the language defined since the end of the 19th century as the Indo-European one, the original matrix of all the languages still spoken on our continent, with the exception of the Basque and Finno-Ugric languages. No newer contribution has, to this very day, come to modify on such a large scale the genetic heritage and linguistic identity of almost all European peoples. The main ethnocultural groups of ancient Europe mostly stem from this common crucible: indeed, regardless of whether one is focusing on ancient Greece and Rome, Germanic peoples, Celts, Balts or Slavs, all are, to varying degrees, bearers of the Indo-European heritage, in combination with more ancient substrata.

Paleogenetic facts thus converge to a large extent with those of linguistics, archeology and history. It should be noted that the modern European peoples whose language does not belong to the Indo-European family (the Basques, Hungarians, Finns, and Estonians) also have roots that reach deep into ancient substrata and have been part of the civilisational framework of Christian Europe for centuries, a framework inherited to a large extent from the Roman imperial world. In the absence of political unity, therefore, Europe's geographical space clearly coincides with the existence of a group of peoples closely related in terms of origin, culture and customs.

This digression along the path of Europe's most ancient past takes us directly to the very heart of our current topic. In contrast with the quixotic notion of individuals endowed with a 'self-shaping' capacity

---

6   AN: For a summary of recent research on the subject, see David Reich's *Who We Are and How We Got There*, translated from the English language by Mathilde Fontanet, Quanto, Lausanne, 2019.

and having an absolute right to free themselves from biological, hereditary and community-related conditioning, one had better remember that man is, first and foremost, a 'social and political animal', one whose profound nature is determined by the twofold heritage passed down by those who preceded it: on the one hand, the bequeathal of a language and a culture and, on the other, that of a genetic heritage. On a collective scale, this dual heritage embodies the identity of a people, alongside the customs and worldview connected with it. Thus, a particular human 'type' is formed, shaped by history in a specific geographical space. It is the feeling of identifying with a given human 'type', with the bearer of a specific culture, that unites the members of a community through the bonds of solidarity that stem from *philia* (φιλία), a notion 'which clearly expresses not a sentimental relationship, but one's belonging to a certain social group'.[7] The awareness of a common origin thus represents the foundation on which the City is erected.

This conception of identity does *not* lead us to freeze our history, centring it on a model that remains immutable, unlike what is claimed by those who denounce the misguided ways of so-called 'essentialism'. Dominique Venner responded masterfully to this objection when he defined tradition as 'a whisper of ancient and future times', as 'that which perseveres and crosses time itself'. For it is not limited to the past, but on the contrary represents 'that which does not pass'. 'It comes to us from the most distant times, yet is still relevant. It is our inner compass.' Identity is a potential that we are to realise in harmony with modalities that remain specific to the contingencies of the moment, so as to attune ourselves to our destiny.

Indeed, the peoples of Europe are the bearers of a specific ethnic and cultural heritage and have every right to want to transmit this heritage across the geographical space that they have shaped for

---

7   AN: Pierre Chantraine, *Dictionnaire étymologique de la langue grecque* [TN: Etymological Dictionary of the Greek Language], Klincksieck, Paris, 1980, p. I 204.

themselves in accordance with their own capabilities and within the civilisational framework that is theirs, particularly through the establishment of the traditional family, which acts as the guardian of our memory and heredity. And it is this fundamental right that we demand for our peoples, a right that Pope Francis readily acknowledges when it comes to Amazonian tribes but denies to Europeans, who are being told to open their doors without any resistance whatsoever. Just like individuals, peoples can also be unfaithful to their heritage, forgetting or rejecting it, as attested by many contemporary examples: this is undoubtedly not the surest way to fulfil one's destiny with honour or even happiness, for that matter. Are we still, however, fully aware of what a people is? In order to clarify and strengthen our understanding of this essential concept, it is necessary, once again, to return to the Greeks.

Ethnos: A Complex Reality

In the ancient Greek world, three terms applied to the notion of 'people': *laos*, *demos*, and *ethnos*. Let us examine the etymology of these words to grasp their deeper meaning.

The term *laos* (ƒÉ.ƒÍ.), related to the Hittite lāḫḫ, i.e. 'campaign', 'war expedition', originally referred to a 'crowd of armed men'. By extension, it takes on the meaning of 'people', as in the expression *Achaiov laos* (Ἀχαιῶν λαός), meaning 'the Achaean people' in the *Iliad*.

As for the term *demos* (δῆμος), it is probably derived from the Indo-European root *deh- ('to divide'), and designates both a portion of a territory and those who inhabit it. By extension, *demos* also refers to a people when considered as a group of individuals that share the same social status or belong to the same city. The corresponding Latin word is *populus*, from which the French word 'peuple' actually comes.

The term *ethnos*, whose etymology expresses the notion of belonging (see above, Chapter I), designates a people as a group sharing a common origin. The same word can also be applied to the animal kingdom, as in the expression *thêrôv ethnê* (Θηρῶν ἔθνη), i.e. 'the races of wild beasts' mentioned by Sophocles: it is therefore a category based on the observation of 'natural' data and not on the result of a 'political' process, as in the case of the *demos*. The *ethnos* represents the people when regarded as a group of families and clans (cf. the Greek *genos* or the Latin *gens*, from the Indo-European root *ǵenhı-, 'to produce', 'to give birth to') that are united by the same 'long history'.

It should also be noted that the distinction between the notions of 'armed people' and people in the 'ethnic' sense also surfaces in the Germanic world. Whereas the German word *Volk* derives from the Proto-Germanic *fulka- ('troop'), the ethnonyms *Teutoni* and *Deutsch* stem from the Proto-Germanic *þeudō (cf. Norse *þjóð*, i.e. 'people'), which is in turn derived from the Indo-European root *teuteh, meaning 'tribe'. This root is also well attested in Baltic languages (cf. the Lithuanian *tautà*, meaning 'people') and Celtic languages (cf. the name of the god Teutates,[8] i.e. the 'father of the nation', or that of the mythical people of the Tuatha Dé Danann, the 'people of the goddess Dana').

If the original meaning of the term *laos* refers to the archaic stage of the Achaean world, which was still very close to the social organisational structure of the Indo-European conqueror groups that imposed their domination in successive waves over a large part of the Eurasian continent from the 4th millennium BC onwards, the *demos* concept probably corresponds to the next phase of Greek history, during which the very structures of the City were consolidated: the *demos* is thus a political community that exercises sovereign authority over a given territory. The notions of *laos* and *demos*, however, do share a common characteristic, in that they both apply to social structures, while the concept of *ethnos* refers more specifically to the origin of the human group that it designates, just like the Latin terms *natio* (whose etymology is linked to *natus*, i.e. the perfect of *nascor*: 'to be born', 'to originate from', 'to come from') and *patria* ('the land of the fathers'). The word *natio* ('offspring', 'species', 'kind', or 'brood') is also applied to the domain of biological realities (cf. the expressions *bona natio*,

---

8   TN: Also known as Toutatis or Totates.

meaning 'abundant brood' or 'great fertility', or *nationes apium*, 'bee varieties'), while the word *patria* [*terra*] implies the notion of territory and refers to the country where one was born, a country considered as one's ancestral land, since Latin society, just like all Indo-European civilisations, was based on people's patrilineal descent. The notions of *ethnos* and *demos* are not contradictory: the latter, in fact, embodies the former's access to a higher stage of organisation that bestows upon it a genuine historical destiny.

Does this mean that *ethnos* is identical to the modern notion of 'race'? The etymology of this term, which first appeared in the French language in the form of *rasse* during the 15th century, having probably been taken from the Italian term *razza*, has not been conclusively established. The most likely hypotheses refer to the Latin *radix* ('root' or 'strain'), to an apheresis[9] of the Latin *generatio* ('generation', 'reproduction', or 'begetting'), or even to the Latin *ratio* ('calculation', 'account' or 'system'). In the last case, the word 'race' is said to have been conceived from the very outset as a reference to a system that allows one to classify living beings. It should, however, be noted that the French language also uses the term in the meaning of 'lineage', as seen in the writings of mediaeval scholars when referring to the three royal 'races' of the Merovingian, Carolingian, and Capetian dynasties.

Beginning in the 19th century, scientific positivism led to various attempts to classify the human species into distinct groups, based on an observation of their phenotypes: height; general morphology; facial features; skull shape; skin, eye, and hair pigmentation; etc. The study of races gradually emerged as a discipline in its own right, occupying a prominent position in anthropological studies, while also attracting the interest of both sociologists and historians studying the history of civilisations. Authors such as Georges Vacher de Lapouge, Arthur de Gobineau, and Houston Stewart Chamberlain even developed a genuine kind of historical philosophy in which human races

---

9   TN: In the field of linguistics, apheresis is defined as the omission of the initial sound of a word, as seen with the English example *he's* (instead of *he is*).

were attributed a decisive role in the emergence of great civilisations, whereas interbreeding phenomena were primarily perceived as factors of decline. Following the upheavals of the First World War, this school of thought, combined with the growing influence of hygienist concerns, inspired various forms of political discourse in both Germany and other Western countries (notably England, Scandinavia, and the United States), culminating in the statal racism established by the National Socialist regime in 1933. While certain social systems that were more or less based on a principle of racial segregation did persist in the United States and certain southern African states for several decades after 1945, the mass crimes committed during the Second World War completely discredited any form of political racism, an ideology now formally condemned by national and international law.

In the scientific output of the immediate post-war period, the validity of the study of racial phenotypes was not completely called into question, but it was now confined to the field of physical anthropology, having lost all legitimacy in social and political sciences. Owing to two different reasons, however, progress in genetic research led many scientists to gradually reject the very notion of race: first of all, because no racial classification could demonstrate the existence of human groups with origins completely independent of those characterising other groups, and secondly, because no typology was subject to complete and definitive consensus. Should one adopt a 'broad' conception of race, thus making distinctions between large groups of people ('Caucasian', 'Sub-Saharan African', 'Middle Eastern', 'Asian', 'Oceanian', 'Native American'), or strive to distinguish more restricted groups from one another (in accordance with phenotypes defined as 'Nordic', 'Mediterranean', 'Alpine', etc., on the European continent, for instance)?

In the latter case, we shall see that these categories never correspond to the presence of a strictly homogeneous physical type within a given people (even if the 'Nordic' type, for example, remains naturally dominant among Scandinavians). The study of the human genome also allows us to demonstrate that most of these groups are the result of the interbreeding of earlier groups, such that the identity of peoples stems from a dynamic process and is not synonymous with the emergence of a completely stable type, 'pure' and devoid of any mixture. In the long term, the phenotype (i.e., the set of observable physical characteristics) can be defined as the product of an interaction between the genotype (i.e., the set of information carried by the genetic make-up of individuals) and the environment—be it through a process of natural selection resulting from adaptation to a given geographic environment, or through social selection stemming from cultural criteria. The validity of racial classifications is ultimately reduced to that of abstract categories comparable to what Max Weber called 'ideal types',[10] whose characteristics are only imperfectly reflected in the realities observed at the level of historically attested human groups. Establishing this form of classification is not in itself illegitimate, insofar as the statistical distribution of these 'ideal types' over a given geographical area is likely to provide a fairly detailed overview of the variety of physical types present within a population. However, the boundaries between the different types can fluctuate quite sharply from one classification to another, depending on the criteria used by the scientists who establish them. Furthermore, it appears impossible to define the existence of a people based exclusively on a racial sort of taxonomy, insofar as ethnic identity never results from the definitive crystallisation of an immutable human type, but rather proceeds from a certain evolution over time: in Europe, particularly, the distribution of physical types rarely coincides with the geographical area of different ethnic groups, and observation of phenotypes does not always allow us to grasp the historical complexity of which the genetic heritage of the various populations still bears traces.

---

10   AN: Max Weber, *Essais sur la théorie de la science* [TN: *Essays on the Theory of Science*, a posthumous collection of texts], translated by Julien Freund, Pocket, Paris, 1995.

Ethnos and *Ethos*

Other considerations, just as crucial as one's genetic heritage, also play a role in the genesis of a people and the maintenance of its cohesion. Aspects such as language; territory and geographic environment; a shared history; one's awareness of having a common origin; reference to the same myths; identical religious and worship practices; having the same customs and the same *ethos*, i.e. a specific way of 'being in the world' (*in-der-Welt-sein*, to use the expression coined by Martin Heidegger), are all essential parameters that combine to shape the fragile balance of collective identity, whose historical sustainability also presupposes a type of 'political' organisation that corresponds to a certain manner of exercising sovereignty over a given space.

Proposed by many anthropologists during the last century, the classification of individuals on the basis of their racial phenotypes does not provide a sufficient set of criteria to understand the complex history of European peoples. Nevertheless, any upheaval in the ethnic composition of a population profoundly alters its collective identity, especially when such an upheaval occurs on a large scale within a few generations. The arrival of massive human migration flows from other civilisational areas cannot come about without trauma, both for the uprooted individuals themselves and for the people that welcome them.

This is not just a matter of an often conflict-ridden clash between different cultures, but rather a much more radical phenomenon, one that affects the very substance of the host nation. Assessing the very magnitude of such a disruption and highlighting the risks that it poses with regard to the cohesion of our peoples does not necessarily stem from an 'essentialist' perspective, as claimed by advocates of widespread interbreeding. The utopian visions espoused by these advocates are often belied by reality itself, to the extent that mass migrations are more likely to trigger the emergence of tensions between communities than their merging into a more or less harmonious 'greater whole'.

Acknowledging the fact that the collective identity of a people or nation is the result of a dynamic process and that identity does not correspond to a static history, but, instead, represents the realisation of a constantly evolving potential, does not imply that one actually believes that this potential remains unchanged when demographic balances are suddenly disrupted. Claiming the opposite would amount to denying the existence of peoples and cultures, while simultaneously proclaiming that nations are comprised of endless masses of interchangeable individuals *ad libitum*, all in accordance with various geopolitical developments or the economic necessities of the moment.

More so than the racial taxonomy of traditional physical anthropology, which is limited to categorising the members of the human species according to their phenotypes, without allowing for a sufficiently precise analysis of the evolution of human groups and the history of interbreeding between different populations, genetics does enable us to considerably refine our knowledge in this field.

Advances in genetics also open up fascinating lines of thought with regard to human *ethology*, that is, to the study of the biological foundations of human behaviour. Now, belonging to a given civilisation is manifested specifically through a particular *ethos*, through a specific way of 'approaching' the world and perceiving it, which one might readily think is not exclusively the result of education and social constraint, but also stems from the transmission—and the slow sedimentation—of certain hereditary predispositions. In any case, the etymological affinities between the words *ethnos* and *ethos* appear eminently significant and not accidental.

Indeed, *ethnos* is much more than a strictly biological notion, for its existence rests upon a shared memory and tradition, as well as upon one's loyalty to a specific *ethos*. And it is the very disappearance of this memory and the denial of this *ethos* that make us vulnerable, much more so than the arrival of entire migration waves on European soil, simply because these waves are not the actual cause of our forgetting and denial, but only their consequence. Reclaiming our lost awareness of our own *ethnos* is, first and foremost, synonymous with conforming to our own *ethos*. The ethics in question obviously belong to a completely different plane than that of universal morality, human rights and the 'values' of the republic, none of which tell us anything about 'what we are'.

In ancient Greek, the word ethos (ἦθος) originally referred to a habitual abode, a den, or the pasture of an animal (notably with Homer). Afterwards, it was applied to the dispositions of the soul, to one's character; Heraclitus taught, for instance,, that 'the character of man bears the mark of a divine power': *êthos anthrôpôi daimôn* (ἦθος ἀνθρώπῳ δαίμων). Last but not least, the same term is used in connection with customs and morals. Just like the word *ethnos*, the Greek term *ethos* has an Indo-European root (*swe-dʰhɪ-, i.e. 'to make one's own', cf. Chapter I) from which the Old High German *sito* and the German *Sitte*, meaning 'customs' or 'morals', are also derived.

Etymologically, ethics therefore designates a way of behaving in accordance with local conventions, customs, and traditions. It is the way in which people behave in relation to the world, in their habitual abode. This link between the notions of custom, abode, and conduct can also be found in the etymological similarity between the French terms 'habitation', 'habitude', and 'habit', all of which relate to the Latin term *habitus*, i.e. one's 'way of being'. The Latin word that most closely corresponds to the Greek *ethos*, however, is *mos*, meaning 'morals', 'customs', and 'conventions', with *mos majorum* ('ancestral customs') having served as the very basis of the morality espoused by the Roman citizen of the classical period. By means of the Latin term *moralis*, the French word *morale* also derives from it.

To rediscover the path to a European *ethos* is to return to the awareness of what we are, while also reclaiming our traditions. This approach is therefore primarily spiritual in nature: it involves a reconsolidation of our common existence in the awareness of what constitutes the very essence of tradition. The notion of essence should not be understood here as an immutable form of absoluteness, but rather as the specific manner in which the being of every single thing unfolds: essence is thus linked to becoming, in accordance with Heraclitus's phrase *Panta rhei* (Πάντα ῥεῖ), meaning 'everything changes'. The essence of a people is therefore the particular way in which it implements its existence on its own territory.

'Become what you are, once you have learned what that is': such is the injunction formulated in the fifth century BC by the Greek poet Pindar, a notion that Nietzsche would later adopt. We must therefore first relearn what our own identity consists of by freeing ourselves from all the illusions generated by the universalistic humanism of the Enlightenment. Through this awareness, we must then seek to once again 'become' what we are, i.e. to affirm our essence through a common existence as a people endowed with a historical destiny on our own territory: for it is by conforming to our *ethos* that we shall one day enable our *ethnos* to reconstitute a City (*polis*) — in other words, to equip itself with a 'political' form that is in keeping with its own genius.

CONCLUSION

RE-BECOMING WHAT WE ARE

CARL SCHMITT defines the 'friend/foe' distinction as the 'criterion of politics', one that mirrors the distinctions established between the beautiful and the ugly, the good and the evil, and the useful and the harmful, all of which prove decisive in the fields of aesthetics, morality, and economics.[1] Without questioning the relevance of this approach, it is also possible to consider that the quintessential political founding act, i.e. the very essence of politics, lies rather in the awareness and affirmation of a given identity and sovereignty than in the designation of one's enemy, which is merely a corollary linked to particular contingencies.

How, then, can we define our specific way of being, our own *ethos*? Shouldn't we, moreover, be wary of ourselves in this regard? Can't Europeans be specifically criticised for having manifested, since the very beginning of the modern era, a 'universalistic' tropism that destroys identities, alongside a desire for power paired with technological domination, the disastrous consequences of which now burden our contemporary world? No longer does the modern reign of technology have anything to do with *techne* (τέχνη) in the Greek sense, which

---

1 AN: Carl Schmitt, *The Notion of the Political*, translated by Marie-Louise Steinhauser, Flammarion, Paris, 1992, page 63.

designates the work of human hands and the mastery of a certain know-how (see also the Latin *ars*). On the contrary, it is but a vision of the world in which reality is reduced to its 'calculable' and rational dimension, and the earth to an 'exploitable resource'. Nature (*physis*) is then 'objectified', i.e. reduced to the status of an object. From this perspective, the history of the world's Westernisation merges, as clearly perceived by Martin Heidegger, with the spread of the 'metaphysics of the unlimited', whose excesses constitute the ultimate driving force of modernity. This is based on the establishment of a 'frame' (*Gestell*) for the appropriation of matter, brought about by an unfathomable 'forgetfulness of being' (*Seinsvergessenheit*). Technology is therefore profoundly ambiguous in itself. It certainly enabled the rise of the European *imperium* across all continents from the 16th century onwards, yet it also represents the irrepressible movement that now leads to a genuinely destructive predation of nature. Technology has thus become fully 'autonomous', having gained its independence from the founding framework of European civilisation, in such manner that the process of Westernisation ceases to be combined with the expansion of European power, imposing instead a type of technological imperialism at the very heart of our civilisation, largely to the latter's detriment.

Did this disastrous development actually begin with the Industrial Revolution, the child of the Enlightenment, or does it stem from more distant times with the emergence of Platonic metaphysics, often considered an attempt to devalue reality in favour of the supernatural sphere? Without becoming involved in this philosophical debate, it seems clear that what has long contributed to our greatness ultimately threatens to lay us in ruin. It is all too clear that the universal liberal values on which the West now claims to exclusively base its identity guarantee the irreversible destruction of our culture and peoples. It therefore appears urgent to 'de-Westernise' our minds and return to the sources of our uniquely European genius. It is not a matter of renouncing the power of technology, which would be a meaningless act and would amount to Europe definitively exiting history, but rather one of re-establishing our vision of technology within a traditional hierarchy of values, subordinating the former to higher ends in the organisation of our societies.

Salvation lies neither in the headlong rush implemented by the liberal model, nor in a retreat towards a kind of 'non-political' idealism. Given the current challenges, we have no other choice but to 'ride the tiger'. To achieve this, it is more necessary than ever to rediscover our taste for power, lost by those whom Nietzsche, in his *Zarathustra*, labels the 'last men' and of whom the ideologists now governing our European institutions are the perfect representatives. This reclaimed appetite for power must, however, also be combined with a rejection of excess—a form of madness that the Greeks called *hubris* (ὕβρις), the daughter of night and the underworld. To the ancients, excess corresponded to a profound transgression of the sacred based on the rejection of natural order, its limits and its hierarchies. In their eyes, it represented the most absolute form of recklessness, one that drives man to seek rivalry with the gods.

It is up to us to replace our desire to 'always have more' with the logic of 'always doing better'. Renouncing the perspective through which the earth is regarded as an inexhaustible resource whose unbridled exploitation would allow us to maintain a trajectory of infinite growth and progress, let us instead adopt the words of Friedrich Hölderlin that 'man dwells as a poet', so that the world may gradually become for us what Martin Heidegger termed 'the fourfold' (*Geviert*): 'the gathering of earth, sky, mortals, and divinities'. But how are we to regain this necessary sense of proportion, combined with a sense of our own strength? Have we not, like the exiles of Corcyra in Thucydides' *Peloponnesian War* (chapter LXXXV, 2-4), definitively 'burned our ships', to such an extent that it would be impossible for us to return to our native shores? In truth, what is needed is not a return to the past; it is not a matter of cultivating nostalgia for a bygone age or the memory of a hypothetical golden age, nor of seeking refuge in some ivory tower. It is rather a question of wresting the minds of our contemporaries from their current torpor, of freeing them from the lies that paralyse them, and of awakening their energies to advance along the path in complete lucidity, while also avoiding the abyss.

As Dominique Venner reminds us in his *Samurai of the West*, 'the upheavals of our time have causes that reach beyond the sole forces of politics or social reforms. It is not enough to change laws or replace one minister with another to establish order where chaos reigns. So as to change behaviours [...], we must reform minds, a task that must always be started anew'. Ever faithful to our 'long European memory', Venner encourages us to respect the triad of Homeric principles: 'nature as the foundation, excellence as the goal, beauty as the horizon'.

The Greeks of the Classical period also offer us a model of the accomplished man, described as 'beautiful and good' (καλὸς κἀγαθός) and able to act appropriately under the gaze of the gods and his peers alike, fulfilling his duties to the City in an exemplary manner. These were also the virtues expected of the Roman citizen: virtues in the sense of the Latin *virtus*, a term designating the qualities that a man (*vir*) must possess. These have been present in constantly renewed forms throughout European history, embodied notably by the figures of the mediaeval knight and the modern gentleman. The Roman example also teaches us the eminently political nature of such an ethic, one that remains inseparable from *pietas*, that is, from the duty rendered to both gods and family, to which one's service to the state is also added. To conform to such an ethic today is to avoid complacency and refuse to abandon oneself to self-aggrandizement, excess, vulgarity, intellectual laziness, conformism, or lack of courage. It is ultimately a question of knowing how to 'conduct oneself' and give shape to one's existence. This is the surest way to shine, awaken, and transmit things within those communities wherein the soul of our peoples still finds expression.

This European *ethos* cannot endure without relying on natural communities (particularly families), on 'social' communities (which aim to perpetuate ancient traditions or to foster, in novel ways, a shared understanding of collective identity), as well as on political communities (particularly at the 'local' level, where specific solidarity and a territorial base conducive to the development of deep-rooted ways of life still persist).

To enable Europeans to emerge from the state of numbness and self-forgetfulness into which the traumas of the 20th century have plunged them, it is more necessary than ever to return to a conception of political order that reconciles the ethnic nation (*ethnos*) and the civic nation (*polis*). This requires a genuine 'intellectual and moral reform', to borrow the title of a famous work by Renan, in which the author notably castigates 'bourgeois materialism, which asks only to peacefully enjoy its acquired wealth'. In the same book, Renan unequivocally condemns the illusions of revolutionary egalitarianism and emphasises the fact that 'the soul of a nation cannot be preserved without a body officially tasked with its protection'.[2] It is towards the establishment of such a 'body' that we must strive. Under the current circumstances, this body must take on the shape of a vanguard ready to venture boldly into an uncertain future, without ever losing sight of the course to follow and always displaying audacity and lucidity, virility and wisdom, in accordance with the exhortation addressed by Duke William to his knights on the morning of the Battle of Hastings.

Calling for the reconciliation of the *ethnos* and the *polis* does not imply inciting people to engage in violent confrontation against a particular community of exogenous origin, even if the deterioration of national cohesion does unfortunately portend, in many Western European countries, an imminent outbreak of crises of considerable intensity. A reappropriation of identity in the civic sphere does not, in itself, stem from a desire to divide the nation, because the responsibility for such 'secession' rests upon the shoulders of the authorities that have allowed the worsening of ethnic, economic and social divides, the magnitude of which we are only just beginning to apprehend.

---

2   AN: Ernest Renan, *La Réforme intellectuelle et morale* [TN: Intellectual and Moral reform], Michel Levy, Paris, 1874.

Reconciling *ethnos* and *polis*, on the other hand, means acknowledging the emptiness of any discourse based on universal 'humanistic' values; it is synonymous with wanting to reroot our peoples in an awareness of common memory. It implies a reaffirmation of our attachment to the same mores and our loyalty to the same *ethos*, a refusal to renounce our ethno-cultural identity. It also means viewing the State as not necessarily destined to become a 'cold monster', one that takes on the shape of a techno-structure that threatens to deprive the nation of its roots, erasing even the slightest memory of an ancestral fatherland now replaced by an 'ideological homeland'. As a sovereign authority governing its own territory, a State must instead embody the very essence of the people from which it emanates, giving it a 'political' expression, which is the only legitimate way to conceive of genuine democracy, the very principle of which is not necessarily the same as the current form of so-called 'democratic' and liberal institutions. Once again, drawing on the longer memory of European peoples could allow us to rediscover a sound conception of social and political order based on the coordination of the three 'functions' of Indo-European tradition: spiritual and legal sovereignty, power, and prosperity. This is not, of course, a question of advocating a return to the institutional model of the three 'orders' of the *Ancien Régime*: indeed, tri-functional conceptions have not systematically led to the establishment of a set of castes based on these three principles in all cultures emerging from the Indo-European melting pot. Much more than a means of political organisation, Indo-European 'tri-functionality' expresses a worldview according to which the inseparable union of the three 'functions' guarantees the harmony of divine order and human societies. It is also important to be aware of the hierarchical nature characterising the intrinsic complementarity between these functions: although sovereignty, power, and prosperity are indeed inseparable, the first function prevails over the other two, just as political ends govern the use of force and are based on economic realities, never allowing 'market' logic, for instance, to spill out of its own sphere and impose itself on all other areas of society.

Conclusion. Re-becoming What We Are

Nowadays, numerous threats are gathering on the horizon, making the prospect of a convergence of catastrophes increasingly likely in the coming decades: an exacerbation of geopolitical tensions, an exponential worsening of demographic imbalances, a depletion of resources paired with environmental degradation caused by a frenetic race towards growth, entry into a phase of recurring economic crises, a trail of social upheavals that such a development inevitably entails, the disintegration of our societies under the dual effect of the subversion of civilisational benchmarks and the loss of ethnic cohesion, and the global vulnerability of these same 'complex' societies, now faced with the risk of major turmoil of either technological or health-related origin. The possibility of facing a series of large-scale upheavals that would radically call into question the very sustainability of the Western liberal model appears increasingly real. It is important to anticipate this timeline, so that the collapse of this model does not drag European peoples down with it nor precipitate them towards a definitive exit from history.

The coming upheavals must, on the contrary, become an opportunity for us to seize the *kairos*, the auspicious and decisive moment from which the 'return to the fatherland' (*vaterländische Umkehr*) mentioned by Hölderlin in his 'Remarks on Antigone' can arise. It shall be a time when European peoples return to a keen awareness of their own destiny, having freed themselves from the illusions that have long blinded them and still paralyse them today.

The mission of the European vanguard mentioned earlier is the following: to prepare us for such a turning point, which shall mark our entry into a new historical cycle characterised by the advent of new forms of political and social organisation, whose future emergence none can nowadays predict. On this level, the notion of European identity does not refer to a mere abstraction, but is embodied in the specific *ethnos* of each of our peoples. Over the course of the modern era, the historical existence of these peoples has gradually taken on the shape of the nation-state, often in a centralising manner. It is not impossible, however, that thanks to the upheavals to come, our ancient fatherlands may, one day, reconnect everywhere with the spirit of earlier traditions, founded on the subsidiarity of organic communities: families, constitutional bodies, municipalities, regions, and the State.[3]

The time that separates us from this decisive turning point can be perceived as a time of transition and uncertainty, during which clear-sighted Europeans will have to rebuild community networks firmly anchored to their territories, without, however, retreating from what remains of the existence of current political, scientific, economic, and social institutions. Condemned to the narrow path of excellence, they will have to learn how to handle the various instruments of power in all areas where they can exert their influence, without ever losing, nor selling, their souls. Above all, they must, just like Dominique Venner in *A Samurai of the West*, cultivate within themselves 'an indestructible faith in the permanence of European tradition', doing so 'every day, like an inaugural invocation'.

---

3   AN: In this regard, it would be most useful to consult the work of German legal historian Otto von Gierke on the concept of *Genossenschaft* ('association') in mediaeval Europe (see in particular: *Political Theories of the Middle Ages*, translated by Jean de Pange, Tenin, Paris, 1914).

L'INSTITUT ILIADE FOR LONG EUROPEAN MEMORY

L'Institut Iliade for Long European Memory, based in France, was born from an observation. Europe is but a shadow of her former self. Replaced by outsiders, confused by having lost their bearing and their pride, Europeans have abandoned the reins of their common destiny to people other than themselves. Europeans no longer remember. Why? Because amongst the current elite — whether at school, university, or in the media — no one passes down to them the cultural wealth of which they are the inheritors.

Contrary to this moribund current, L'Institut Iliade has given itself the task of participating in the renewal of the cultural grandeur of Europe and in aiding Europeans' reappropriation of their own identity. Facing the Great Erasure of culture, we intend to work for the Great Awakening of European consciousness and to help prepare Europe for a new renaissance — one of identity, freedom, and power.

L'Institut Iliade's calling is threefold:

- To train young men and young women concerned about their history to always build. To make them the avantgarde of the renaissance for which the Institut calls: men and women capable of giving to civic and political action that cultural and metapolitical dimension which is indispensable. Their motto: to put themselves at the service of a community of destiny, which risks disappearing if it is not taken in hand. Armed with a strong culture relating to European traditions and values, they learn to discern that the adventure that awaits them entails risks and self-sacrifice, but also enthusiasm and joy.

- To promote a radical and alternative vision of the world contrary to the dogmas of universalism, egalitarianism, and 'diversity'. Using all available means, the Institut develops concepts and ammunition to understand and fight the modern world.

- To gather together, especially — but not only — in France, those who refuse to submit and who are inspired daily by the Homeric triad as described by Dominique Venner: nature as the base, excellence as the goal, beauty as the horizon.

L'Institut Iliade's originality, especially with the aim of reformulating and updating knowledge, lies in tying together the seriousness of its content with ease of learning for the greater public, the objective being to demonstrate an authentic pedagogy, and to act in complementary or supportive ways with other initiatives having the same goal.

L'Institut Iliade's action takes place across various channels:

- A cadre school of the European Rebirth, which every year brings together trainees from a wide variety of backgrounds and is already seeing citizens from other European countries participate;
- an annual colloquium — made up of academics, politicians, writers, journalists, and association officials from all over Europe — that meets in Paris to discuss strong and challenging themes, such as 'The Aesthetic Universe of Europeans', 'Facing the Migratory Assault', 'Transmit or Disappear', 'Nature as Base — for an Ecology of Place', 'Beyond the Market — Economy at the Service of Peoples';

- the publication of works — designed as beacons to enlighten readers' thoughts and guide them toward the reconquest of their identity — within several collections, made available in the widest array of languages and European countries;
- artistic exhibitions on the fringes of contemporary artistic trends, allowing the public to take a fresh look at art and rooted creation;
- an incubator for ideas, businesses, and associations to support and help the greatest number of projects — with quality and sustainability criteria — across all fields of civil society (culture, commerce, etc.) that seek to impose a rooted vision of the world and an alternative to the current system, while prioritising structures and projects making an impact in real life;
- an active presence on social media, allowing us to reach new audiences (through videos, publications, annual events, and news presentations), centred around a website that functions as much as a resource hub as it does as a platform for exchanges and debate, notably offering an ideal library of more than five hundred works, a European primer, a dictionary of quotations, and turnkey itineraries for visiting and hiking the prominent places of European memory.

Education through history:

L'Institut Iliade endeavours to uphold in every circumstance the richness and singularity of our heritage in order to draw forth the source and the resources of a serene, but determined, affirmation of our identity, both national and European. In line with the thought and deeds of Dominique Venner, the Institut accords in all its activities an essential place to history, both as a matrix of deep meditation on the future as well as a place of the unexpected, where anything is possible.

Concerning Europe, it seems as though we will be forced to rise up and face immense challenges and fearsome catastrophes even beyond those posed by immigration. These hardships will present the opportunity for both a rebirth and a rediscovery of ourselves. I believe in those qualities that are specific to the European people, qualities currently in a state of dormancy. I believe in our active individuality, our inventiveness, and in the awakening of our energy. This awakening will undoubtedly come. When? I do not know, but I am positive that it will take place.

— Dominique Venner, *The Shock of History*
Arktos Media, London, 2015

Follow L'Institut Iliade at
www.institut-iliade.com
linktr.ee/InstitutILIADE

OTHER BOOKS PUBLISHED BY ARKTOS

Virginia Abernethy	*Born Abroad*
Sri Dharma Pravartaka Acharya	*The Dharma Manifesto*
Joakim Andersen	*Rising from the Ruins*
Winston C. Banks	*Excessive Immigration*
Stephen Baskerville	*Who Lost America?*
Alfred Baeumler	*Nietzsche: Philosopher and Politician*
Matt Battaglioli	*The Consequences of Equality*
Alain de Benoist	*Beyond Human Rights*
	Carl Schmitt Today
	The Ideology of Sameness
	The Indo-Europeans
	Manifesto for a European Renaissance
	On the Brink of the Abyss
	The Problem of Democracy
	Runes and the Origins of Writing
	View from the Right (vol. 1–3)
Armand Berger	*Tolkien, Europe, and Tradition*
Pawel Bielawski	*European Apostasy*
Arthur Moeller van den Bruck	*Germany's Third Empire*
Kerry Bolton	*The Perversion of Normality*
	Revolution from Above
	Yockey: A Fascist Odyssey
Isac Boman	*Money Power*
Charles William Dailey	*The Serpent Symbol in Tradition*
Antoine Dresse	*Political Realism*
Ricardo Duchesne	*Faustian Man in a Multicultural Age*
Alexander Dugin	*Ethnos and Society*
	Ethnosociology
	Eurasian Mission
	The Fourth Political Theory
	The Great Awakening vs the Great Reset
	Last War of the World-Island
	Politica Aeterna
	Political Platonism
	Putin vs Putin
	The Rise of the Fourth Political Theory
	The Trump Revolution
	Templars of the Proletariat
	The Theory of a Multipolar World
Daria Dugina	*A Theory of Europe*
Edward Dutton	*Race Differences in Ethnocentrism*
Mark Dyal	*Hated and Proud*
Clare Ellis	*The Blackening of Europe*
Koenraad Elst	*Return of the Swastika*
Julius Evola	*The Bow and the Club*
	Fascism Viewed from the Right
	A Handbook for Right-Wing Youth
	Metaphysics of Power

OTHER BOOKS PUBLISHED BY ARKTOS

	Metaphysics of War
	The Myth of the Blood
	Notes on the Third Reich
	Pagan Imperialism
	Recognitions
	A Traditionalist Confronts Fascism
GUILLAUME FAYE	*Archeofuturism*
	Archeofuturism 2.0
	The Colonisation of Europe
	Convergence of Catastrophes
	Ethnic Apocalypse
	A Global Coup
	Prelude to War
	Sex and Deviance
	Understanding Islam
	Why We Fight
DANIEL S. FORREST	*Suprahumanism*
ANDREW FRASER	*Dissident Dispatches*
	Reinventing Aristocracy in the Age of Woke Capital
	The WASP Question
GÉNÉRATION IDENTITAIRE	*We are Generation Identity*
PETER GOODCHILD	*The Taxi Driver from Baghdad*
	The Western Path
PAUL GOTTFRIED	*War and Democracy*
PETR HAMPL	*Breached Enclosure*
PORUS HOMI HAVEWALA	*The Saga of the Aryan Race*
CONSTANTIN VON HOFFMEISTER	*Esoteric Trumpism*
	MULTIPOLARITY!
RICHARD HOUCK	*Liberalism Unmasked*
A. J. ILLINGWORTH	*Political Justice*
INSTITUT ILIADE	*For a European Awakening*
	Guardians of Heritage
ALEXANDER JACOB	*De Naturae Natura*
JASON REZA JORJANI	*Artemis Unveiled*
	Closer Encounters
	Erosophia
	Faustian Futurist
	Iranian Leviathan
	Lovers of Sophia
	Metapolemos
	Novel Folklore
	Philosophy of the Future
	Prometheism
	Promethean Pirate
	Prometheus and Atlas
	Psychotron
	Uber Man
	World State of Emergency
HENRIK JONASSON	*Sigmund*

OTHER BOOKS PUBLISHED BY ARKTOS

EDGAR JULIUS JUNG	*The Significance of the German Revolution*
RUUBEN KAALEP & AUGUST MEISTER	*Rebirth of Europe*
RODERICK KAINE	*Smart and SeXy*
JAMES KIRKPATRICK	*Conservatism Inc.*
LUDWIG KLAGES	*The Biocentric Worldview*
	Cosmogonic Reflections
	The Science of Character
ANDREW KORYBKO	*Hybrid Wars*
PIERRE KREBS	*Guillaume Faye: Truths & Tributes*
	Fighting for the Essence
JULIEN LANGELLA	*Catholic and Identitarian*
JOHN BRUCE LEONARD	*The New Prometheans*
DIANA PANCHENKO	*The Inevitable*
JEAN-YVES LE GALLOU	*The Propaganda Society*
STEPHEN PAX LEONARD	*The Ideology of Failure*
	Travels in Cultural Nihilism
WILLIAM S. LIND	*Reforging Excalibur*
	Retroculture
PENTTI LINKOLA	*Can Life Prevail?*
GIORGIO LOCCHI	*Definitions*
H. P. LOVECRAFT	*The Conservative*
NORMAN LOWELL	*Imperium Europa*
RICHARD LYNN	*Sex Differences in Intelligence*
	A Tribute to Helmut Nyborg (ed.)
JOHN MACLUGASH	*The Return of the Solar King*
CHARLES MAURRAS	*The Future of the Intelligentsia &*
	For a French Awakening
GRAEME MAXTON	*The Follies of the Western Mind*
JOHN HARMON MCELROY	*Agitprop in America*
MICHAEL O'MEARA	*Guillaume Faye and the Battle of Europe*
	New Culture, New Right
MICHAEL MILLERMAN	*Beginning with Heidegger*
DMITRY MOISEEV	*The Philosophy of Italian Fascism*
MAURICE MURET	*The Greatness of Elites*
BRIAN ANSE PATRICK	*The NRA and the Media*
	Rise of the Anti-Media
	The Ten Commandments of Propaganda
	Zombology
TITO PERDUE	*The Bent Pyramid*
	Journey to a Location
	Lee
	Morning Crafts
	Philip
	The Sweet-Scented Manuscript
	William's House (vol. 1–4)
JOHN K. PRESS	*The True West vs the Zombie Apocalypse*

OTHER BOOKS PUBLISHED BY ARKTOS

Raido	*A Handbook of Traditional Living* (vol. 1–2)
P R Reddall	*Towards Awakening*
Claire Rae Randall	*The War on Gender*
Steven J. Rosen	*The Agni and the Ecstasy*
	The Jedi in the Lotus
Nicholas Rooney	*Talking to the Wolf*
Richard Rudgley	*Barbarians*
	Essential Substances
	Wildest Dreams
Ernst von Salomon	*It Cannot Be Stormed*
	The Outlaws
Werner Sombart	*Traders and Heroes*
Piero San Giorgio	*Giuseppe*
	Survive the Economic Collapse
	Surviving the Next Catastrophe
Sri Sri Ravi Shankar	*Celebrating Silence*
	Know Your Child
	Management Mantras
	Patanjali Yoga Sutras
	Secrets of Relationships
Oswald Spengler	*The Decline of the West*
	Man and Technics
Richard Storey	*The Uniqueness of Western Law*
J. R. Sommer	*The New Colossus*
Tomislav Sunic	*Against Democracy and Equality*
	Homo Americanus
	Postmortem Report
	Titans are in Town
Askr Svarte	*Gods in the Abyss*
Hans-Jürgen Syberberg	*On the Fortunes and Misfortunes of Art in Post-War Germany*
Abir Taha	*Defining Terrorism*
	The Epic of Arya (2nd ed.)
	Nietzsche is Coming God, or the Redemption of the Divine
	Verses of Light
Jean Thiriart	*Europe: An Empire of 400 Million*
Bal Gangadhar Tilak	*The Arctic Home in the Vedas*
Dominique Venner	*Ernst Jünger: A Different European Destiny*
	For a Positive Critique
	The Shock of History
Hans Vogel	*How Europe Became American*
Markus Willinger	*A Europe of Nations*
	Generation Identity
Alexander Wolfheze	*Alba Rosa*
	Globus Horribilis
	Rupes Nigra

www.ingramcontent.com/pod-product-compliance
Lightning Source LLC
Chambersburg PA
CBHW051703040426
42446CB00009B/1269